Facts About the Hyena (Spotted)

By Lisa Strattin

© 2019 Lisa Strattin

Facts for Kids Picture Books by Lisa Strattin

Ladybugs and Fireflies, Vol 1

Squids Will Be Squids, Vol 2

Manx Cats, Vol 3

Chipmunks, Vol 5

Hummingbirds, Vol 7

African Elephants, Vol 8

American Alligators, Vol 9

Anaconda, Vol 11

Blue and Gold Macaw, Vol 13

Burrowing Owl, Vol 18

Sign Up for New Release Emails Here

http://LisaStrattin.com/subscribe-here

Monthly Surprise Box

http://KidCraftsByLisa.com

Contents

INTRODUCTION

These Spotted Hyenas have a great reputation as being bad villains wherever they live. Because of the sound this animal makes, it has attained the popular name of being called the Laughing Hyena. The Sub Saharan Africa is the native home of this animal. They are a major predator species and usually have no worry of food.

CHARACTERISTICS

Spotted Hyenas are social and prefer living in clans of as many as 80 animals. They are totally dependent upon the available prey. For example, in the Serengeti where the prey migrates, the groups are kept smaller in order to make hunting easier. But in the areas where the prey stays in a local habitat all year long, the clans are much more in number.

The life of the clan centers around the den which they call home for many years.

Hyenas show primal intelligence and have evolved even more over the years.

APPEARANCE

The Spotted Hyena has a strong neck; the head is flat and strong as well. The Spotted Hyena has pointed ears. Their feet have 4 toes, and the toes are webbed. The front legs are rather small and appear stout and stunted. The claws are not sharp at all.

Their fur is known to change with age. The spots are darker colors than the rest of their coat. These spots can vary from being red to blackish.

LIFE STAGES

Although the Spotted Hyena is a non-seasonal breeder, there is a burst of breeding during the rainy season. They do not limit themselves to one partner and are known to mate with several partners over their lifetime. Once the female has conceived, she will have a litter of cubs at around 110 days later.

These cubs, at the time of birth, weigh about 3 pounds and have black hairs which are very soft and velvety. After 2 to 3 months, the cubs start shedding their black skins or furs and develop the typical hyena light colored furs.

LIFE SPAN

The average lifespan of a Spotted Hyena is about 12 years, although this number is gathered from hyenas in captivity at zoos. There have been no studies, as of this writing, of how long they live in the wild.

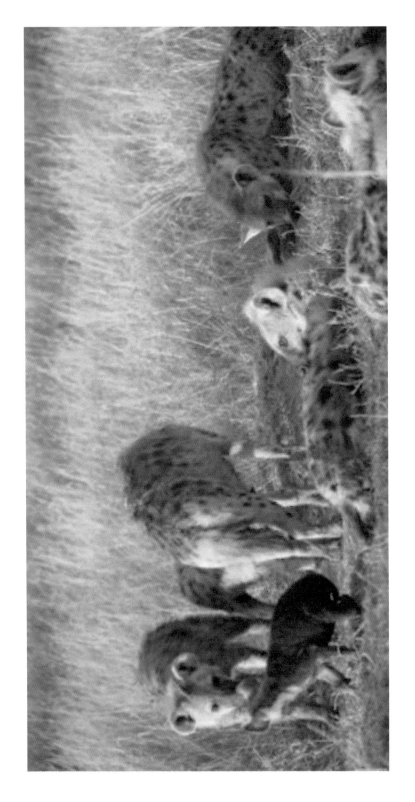

SIZE

The Spotted Hyena is usually between 3 to 5 ½ feet long and they weigh between 85 to 120 pounds on average.

HABITAT

The Spotted Hyena had vast population all over the world and the population has been most significant in the European region in years past. But now most of their numbers live in the areas of Ethiopia, Tanzania, Kenya, and the Botswana areas in Africa.

DIET

The Spotted Hyena is a hardcore carnivore. The Spotted Hyena is not like its other cousins, the striped ones – who are strictly scavengers. It is a proper predator, chasing down live prey for its meal. This has known to feed on wildebeest and buffalo as its major or primary prey. It also feeds on zebras, impala, giraffes and many more good-sized animals.

FRIENDS AND ENEMIES

These are predators and live in clans. They do not have any friendly relationships with other animals. They are enemies of lions, leopards, cheetahs, and African wild dogs.

SUITABILITY AS PETS

The Spotted Hyena is completely unsuitable as a pet. They are strictly meat-eaters and do not get along well with humans.

COLOR ME

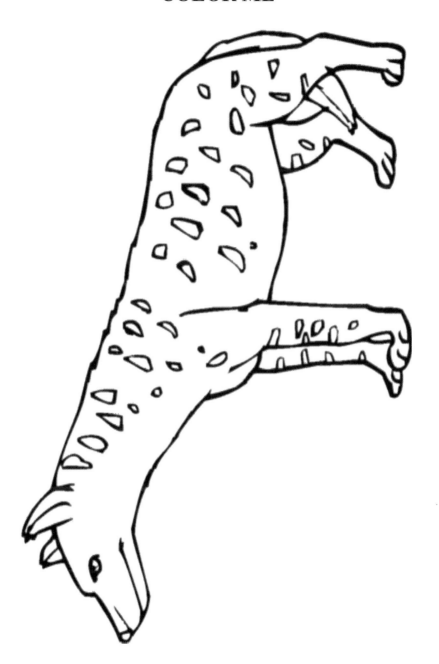

COLOR ME

COLOR ME

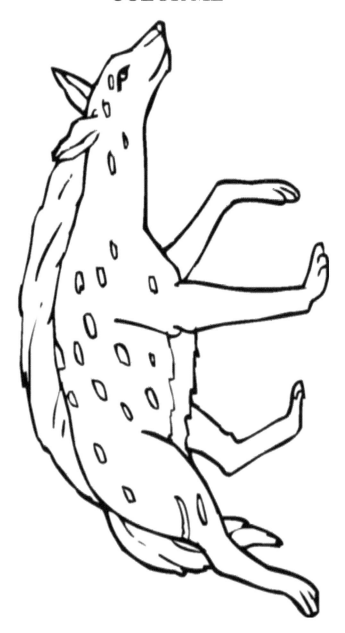

Please leave me a review here:

http://lisastrattin.com/Review-Vol-68

For more Kindle Downloads Visit Lisa Strattin Author Page on Amazon Author Central

http://amazon.com/author/lisastrattin

To see upcoming titles, visit my website at LisaStrattin.com– all books available on kindle!

http://lisastrattin.com

PLUSH HYENA

You can get one by copying and pasting this link into your browser:

http://lisastrattin.com/plushhyena

MONTHLY SURPRISE BOX

Get yours by copying and pasting this link into your browser

http://KidCraftsByLisa.com

Printed in Great Britain
by Amazon

57107122R00022